Checklist

Important addresses & details:

Your Current Address	

Your New Address	
New Phone #	

Agent / Realtor	
Address	
Phone #	
Email	
Website	

Current Landlord	
Address	

Inventory Tracker

Documents	Room	Box	Replacement Estimate
Appliances			
Furniture			
Electronics			

Miscellaneous Items Checklist

General	Check	Cleaning	Check
Desk chair		Cleaning supplies (wipes paper towels, spray)	
Keychain		Air freshener	
Light bulbs		Small vacuum	
Small sewing kit		Dish detergent	
Small tool kit		Dish towel	
First aid kit		Quarters for laundry	
Tissues		Detergent/fabric softener	
Cotton Balls		Hamper/Laundry basket	
Pillow/Blankets		Drying Rack	
Extra-long sheets for dorm beds		Iron/Ironing Board	
Sleep mask/Ear plugs			
Eraser board/Pen		**Bathroom**	
Space heater		Shower caddy	
Fan		Shower shoes	
Alarm clock		Robe	
Flashlight		Towel	
Bug spray		Shampoo/Conditioner	
Umbrella		Soap/Body Wash	
Storage Shelves/Boxes		Razors	
Hangers		Hairdryer/Curling Iron	

Move Out Inspection Checklist

KITCHEN	Condition	Clean/Fix it
Stove/Oven		
Refrigerator		
Sink		
Flooring		
Countertops		
Cabinets		
LIVING ROOM		
Flooring		
Walls		
Light Fixtures		
Windows		
BEDROOM 1		
Flooring		
Walls		
Light Fixtures		
Windows		
BATHROOM 1		
Countertop		
Tub/Shower		
Flooring		
BEDROOM 2		
Flooring		
Walls		
Light Fixtures		
Windows		

Change of Address Tracker

Name/Company:	
Our address will change as of (date)	

Former Address	New Address
Street:	Street:
City & State	City & State
ZIP code:	ZIP code:

Name/Company:	
Our address will change as of (date)	

Former Address	New Address
Street:	Street:
City & State	City & State
ZIP code:	ZIP code:

Grocery Re-stock Checklist

Fruits
☐ apples
☐ apricots
☐ avocados
☐ bananas
☐ berries
☐ cherries
☐ grapefruit
☐ grapes
☐ kiwi
☐ lemons
☐ limes
☐ melons
☐ nectarines
☐ oranges
☐ papaya
☐ peaches
☐ pears
☐ plums
☐ pomegranate
☐ watermelon
☐ _____
☐ _____
☐ _____

Meat
☐ bacon
☐ chicken
☐ deli meat
☐ ground beef
☐ ground turkey
☐ ham
☐ hot dogs
☐ pork
☐ sausage
☐ steak
☐ turkey
☐ _____

Seafood
☐ catfish
☐ cod
☐ crab
☐ halibut
☐ lobster
☐ oysters
☐ salmon
☐ shrimp

Baking
☐ baking powder
☐ baking soda
☐ bread crumbs
☐ cake decor
☐ cake mix
☐ canned milk
☐ chocolate chips
☐ cocoa
☐ cornmeal
☐ cornstarch
☐ flour
☐ food coloring
☐ frosting
☐ muffin mix
☐ pie crust
☐ shortening
☐ sugar (brown)
☐ sugar (powdered)
☐ sugar
☐ yeast

Pasta & Rice
☐ brown rice
☐ burger helper
☐ couscous
☐ elbow macaroni
☐ lasagna
☐ mac & cheese
☐ noodle mix
☐ rice mix
☐ spaghetti
☐ white rice
☐ _____
☐ _____

Cans & Jars
☐ applesauce
☐ baked beans
☐ black beans
☐ broth
☐ bullion cubes
☐ canned fruit
☐ canned vegetables

Seasoning
☐ basil
☐ bay leaves
☐ BBQ seasoning
☐ cinnamon
☐ cloves
☐ cumin
☐ curry
☐ dill
☐ garlic powder
☐ garlic salt
☐ gravy mix
☐ Italian seasoning
☐ marinade
☐ meat tenderizer
☐ oregano
☐ paprika
☐ pepper
☐ poppy seed
☐ red pepper
☐ sage

Daily Planner

Top Priority

Schedule		Calls
8:00		
8:30		
9:00		
9:30		
10:00		
10:30		
11:00		
11:30		**Miscellaneous**
12:00		

Addtional Notes/Journal Pages

Home Moving Checklist & Contact-List

Important addresses & details:

Your Current Address	
Current Phone #	
Email ID	

Your New Address	
New Phone #	

Agent / Realtor	
Address	
Phone #	
Email	
Website	

Current Landlord	
Address	
Phone #	
Email	

New Landlord / Seller	
Address	
Phone #	
Email	

Packers & Movers	
Address	
Phone #	
Email	
Website	
Customer #	

Moving Insurance	
Address	
Phone #	
Email	
Website	
Reference #	

Electricity	
Address	
Phone #	
Email	
Website	
Customer #	
Turn Off Date	
Pending dues	

Gas Supplier	
Address	
Phone #	
Email	
Website	
Customer #	
Turn Off Date	
Pending dues	

Water Utility	
Address	
Phone #	
Email	
Website	
Customer #	
Turn Off Date	
Pending dues	

Sewerage	
Address	
Phone #	
Email	
Website	
Customer #	
Turn Off Date	
Pending dues	

Garbage Collection	
Address	
Phone #	
Email	
Website	
Customer #	
Turn Off Date	
Pending dues	

DAMN
I Hate *Moving*

Telephone Service	
Address	
Phone #	
Email	
Website	
Customer #	
Turn Off Date	

Mobile Service provider	
Address	
Phone #	
Email	
Website	
Customer #	
Turn Off Date	

Internet Service	
Address	
Phone #	
Email	
Website	
Customer #	
Turn Off Date	

Cable TV	
Address	
Phone #	
Email	
Website	
Customer #	
Turn Off Date	

Gardening	
Address	
Phone #	
Email	
Website	
Customer #	
Stop date	

New Utilities and Services

Electricity	
Address	
Phone #	
Email	
Website	
Customer #	
Turn On Date	

Gas Supplier	
Address	
Phone #	
Email	
Website	
Customer #	
Turn On Date	

Water Utility	
Address	
Phone #	
Email	
Website	
Customer #	
Turn On Date	

Sewage	
Address	
Phone #	
Email	
Website	
Customer #	
Turn On Date	

Garbage Collection	
Address	
Phone #	
Email	
Website	
Customer #	
Start Date	

DAMN
I Hate *Moving*

Telephone	
Address	
Phone #	
Email	
Website	
Customer #	
Turn On Date	

Mobile Service Provider	
Address	
Phone #	
Email	
Website	
Customer #	
Turn On Date	

Internet	
Address	
Phone #	
Email	
Website	
Customer #	
Turn On Date	

Cable TV	
Address	
Phone #	
Email	
Website	
Customer #	
Turn On Date	

Gardening	
Address	
Phone #	
Email	
Website	
Customer #	
Start Date	

Other contacts who need to be informed about your move (Bank, Subscriptions, Friends etc.)

Contact name & address	
Phone #	
Email ID	

Contact name & address	
Phone #	
Email ID	

Contact name & address	
Phone #	
Email ID	

Contact name & address	
Phone #	
Email ID	

Contact name & address	
Phone #	
Email ID	

Contact name & address	
Phone #	
Email ID	

Contact name & address	
Phone #	
Email ID	

Contact name & address	
Phone #	
Email ID	

Contact name & address	
Phone #	
Email ID	

 Moving Inventory Organizer

Documents	Room	Box	Replacement Estimate
Appliances	-	-	-
Furniture	-	-	-
Electronics	-	-	-
Clothing	-	-	-
Entertainment	-	-	-
Repair/Cleaning Materials	-	-	-
Personal Items	-	-	-

Moving Inventory Organizer

Documents	Room	Box	Replacement Estimate
Appliances	-	-	-
Furniture	-	-	-
Electronics	-	-	-
Clothing	-	-	-
Entertainment	-	-	-
Repair/Cleaning Materials	-	-	-
Personal Items	-	-	-

Moving Inventory Organizer

Documents	Room	Box	Replacement Estimate
Appliances	-	-	-
Furniture	-	-	-
Electronics	-	-	-
Clothing	-	-	-
Entertainment	-	-	-
Repair/Cleaning Materials	-	-	-
Personal Items	-	-	-

Moving Inventory Organizer

Documents	Room	Box	Replacement Estimate
Appliances	-	-	-
Furniture	-	-	-
Electronics	-	-	-
Clothing	-	-	-
Entertainment	-	-	-
Repair/Cleaning Materials	-	-	-
Personal Items	-	-	-

Moving Inventory Organizer

Documents	Room	Box	Replacement Estimate
Appliances	-	-	-
Furniture	-	-	-
Electronics	-	-	-
Clothing	-	-	-
Entertainment	-	-	-
Repair/Cleaning Materials	-	-	-
Personal Items	-	-	-

Odd Things Packing Checklist

General	Check	Cleaning	Check
Desk chair		Cleaning supplies (wipes/paper towels, spray)	
Keychain		Air freshener	
Light bulbs		Small vacuum	
Small sewing kit		Dish detergent	
Small tool kit		Dish towel	
First aid kit		Quarters for laundry	
Tissues		Detergent/fabric softener	
Cotton Balls		Hamper/laundry basket	
Pillow/Blankets		Drying Rack	
Extra-long sheets for dorm beds		Iron/Ironing Board	
Sleep mask/Ear plugs			
Eraser board/Pen		**Bathroom**	-
Space heater		Shower caddy	
Fan		Shower shoes	
Alarm clock		Robe	
Flashlight		Towel	
Bug spray		Shampoo/Conditioner	
Umbrella		Soap/Body Wash	
Storage Shelves/Boxes		Razors	
Hangers		Hairdryer/Curling Iron	
Pocket organizers to hang from closets/doors		Brush/Comb	
Posters/Photos/Thumbtacks		Deodorant	
Hat rack		Cosmetics	
Mirror		Toothbrush/Toothpaste/Floss	
Hotplate/Toaster/Microwave		Band-Aids	
Cups/Plates/Bowls/Utensils		Medication	
Bike/Lock/Helmet		Glasses/Case/Cleaner	
		Contact lenses/Case/Cleaner	
Electronics	-	Pain reliever	
TV/Remote		Vitamins	
DVD Player/VCR		Q-Tips	
Gaming Console		Nail clippers/Tweezers	
Cellphone/Charger			
Laptop/Battery/Charger/Case		**Clothing**	-
Laptop lock		Jeans/Slacks/Shorts	
Speakers		T-shirts/Sweatshirts/Tank tops	
Ethernet cable		Socks/Underwear	
Flash drive/External hard drive		Swimsuit	
Power strip/Extension cord		Hats/Belts	
Printer/Paper/Ink		Raincoat/Winter coat/Jacket	
Batteries		Shoes/Boots/Sandals	
Camera		Pajamas	
Stereo/MP3 player		Workout Clothes	
Lamp/Night light		Jewelry/Watch	
Movies/CDs		Dress Clothes	

Use this sheet to self inspect your place. Make sure to take pictures also.

Self Move-Out Inspection

Landlord's Name
Address/Unit #

	Condition	Clean/Fix (Y or N)	Notes
KITCHEN			
Stove/Oven			
Refrigerator			
Sink			
Flooring			
Countertops			
Cabinets			
LIVING ROOM			
Flooring			
Walls			
Light Fixtures			
Windows			
BEDROOM 1			
Flooring			
Walls			
Light Fixtures			
Windows			
BATHROOM 1			
Sink			
Countertop			
Tub/Shower			
Flooring			
BEDROOM 2			
Flooring			
Walls			
Light Fixtures			
Windows			

Don't forget to forward your mail to your new address. If not, you'll need to make sure that you notify anyone who sends you mail of your new address or address you would like to receive mail at. This form can be helpful to keep track of that. Especially, if you are forwarding mail to multiple addresses.

Change of Address

Name/Company:
Our address will change as of (date):

Former Address	New Address
Street:	Street:
City & State:	City & State:
ZIP code:	ZIP code:

Name/Company:
Our address will change as of (date):

Former Address	New Address
Street:	Street:
City & State:	City & State:
ZIP code:	ZIP code:

Name/Company:
Our address will change as of (date):

Former Address	New Address
Street:	Street:
City & State:	City & State:
ZIP code:	ZIP code:

Additional Change of Address

DAMN
I Hate *Moving* Master Grocery List

Fruits
- [ ] apples
- [ ] apricots
- [ ] avocados
- [ ] bananas
- [ ] berries
- [ ] cherries
- [ ] grapefruit
- [ ] grapes
- [ ] kiwi
- [ ] lemons
- [ ] limes
- [ ] melons
- [ ] nectarines
- [ ] oranges
- [ ] papaya
- [ ] peaches
- [ ] pears
- [ ] plums
- [ ] pomegranate
- [ ] watermelon
- [ ] _____
- [ ] _____
- [ ] _____

Vegetables
- [ ] artichokes
- [ ] asparagus
- [ ] basil
- [ ] beets
- [ ] broccoli
- [ ] cabbage
- [ ] cauliflower
- [ ] carrots
- [ ] celery
- [ ] chilies
- [ ] chives
- [ ] cilantro
- [ ] corn
- [ ] cucumbers
- [ ] eggplant
- [ ] garlic cloves
- [ ] green onions
- [ ] lettuce
- [ ] onions
- [ ] peppers
- [ ] potatoes
- [ ] salad greens
- [ ] spinach
- [ ] sprouts
- [ ] squash
- [ ] tomatoes
- [ ] zucchini
- [ ] _____
- [ ] _____
- [ ] _____

Breakfast
- [ ] cereal
- [ ] grits
- [ ] instant breakfast drink
- [ ] oatmeal
- [ ] pancake mix
- [ ] _____
- [ ] _____
- [ ] _____
- [ ] _____

Meat
- [ ] bacon
- [ ] chicken
- [ ] deli meat
- [ ] ground beef
- [ ] ground turkey
- [ ] ham
- [ ] hot dogs
- [ ] pork
- [ ] sausage
- [ ] steak
- [ ] turkey
- [ ] _____
- [ ] _____

Seafood
- [ ] catfish
- [ ] cod
- [ ] crab
- [ ] halibut
- [ ] lobster
- [ ] oysters
- [ ] salmon
- [ ] shrimp
- [ ] tilapia
- [ ] tuna
- [ ] _____

Frozen
- [ ] chicken bites
- [ ] desserts
- [ ] fish sticks
- [ ] fruit
- [ ] ice
- [ ] ice cream
- [ ] ice pops
- [ ] juice
- [ ] meat
- [ ] pie shells
- [ ] pizza
- [ ] pot pies
- [ ] potatoes
- [ ] TV dinners
- [ ] vegetables
- [ ] veggie burger
- [ ] waffles
- [ ] _____
- [ ] _____
- [ ] _____

Baby
- [ ] baby cereal
- [ ] baby food
- [ ] diapers
- [ ] diaper cream
- [ ] formula
- [ ] wipes
- [ ] _____

Pets
- [ ] cat food
- [ ] cat sand
- [ ] dog food
- [ ] shampoo
- [ ] treats
- [ ] flea treatment
- [ ] _____

Baking
- [ ] baking powder
- [ ] baking soda
- [ ] bread crumbs
- [ ] cake decor
- [ ] cake mix
- [ ] canned milk
- [ ] chocolate chips
- [ ] cocoa
- [ ] cornmeal
- [ ] cornstarch
- [ ] flour
- [ ] food coloring
- [ ] frosting
- [ ] muffin mix
- [ ] pie crust
- [ ] shortening
- [ ] sugar (brown)
- [ ] sugar (powdered)
- [ ] sugar
- [ ] yeast
- [ ] _____
- [ ] _____

Snacks
- [ ] candy
- [ ] cookies
- [ ] crackers
- [ ] dried fruit
- [ ] fruit snacks
- [ ] gelatin
- [ ] graham crackers
- [ ] granola bars
- [ ] gum
- [ ] nuts
- [ ] popcorn
- [ ] potato chips
- [ ] pretzels
- [ ] pudding
- [ ] raisins
- [ ] seeds
- [ ] tortilla chips
- [ ] _____
- [ ] _____
- [ ] _____

Bakery
- [ ] bagels
- [ ] bread
- [ ] donuts
- [ ] cake
- [ ] cookies
- [ ] croutons
- [ ] dinner rolls
- [ ] hamburger buns
- [ ] hot dog buns
- [ ] muffins
- [ ] pastries
- [ ] pie
- [ ] pita bread
- [ ] tortillas (corn)
- [ ] tortillas (flour)
- [ ] _____

Pasta & Rice
- [ ] brown rice
- [ ] burger helper
- [ ] couscous
- [ ] elbow macaroni
- [ ] lasagna
- [ ] mac & cheese
- [ ] noodle mix
- [ ] rice mix
- [ ] spaghetti
- [ ] white rice
- [ ] _____
- [ ] _____

Cans & Jars
- [ ] applesauce
- [ ] baked beans
- [ ] black beans
- [ ] broth
- [ ] bullion cubes
- [ ] canned fruit
- [ ] canned vegetables
- [ ] carrots
- [ ] chili
- [ ] corn
- [ ] creamed corn
- [ ] jam/jelly
- [ ] mushrooms
- [ ] olives (green)
- [ ] olives (black)
- [ ] pasta
- [ ] pasta sauce
- [ ] peanut butter
- [ ] pickles
- [ ] pie filling
- [ ] soup
- [ ] _____
- [ ] _____

Refrigerated
- [ ] biscuits
- [ ] butter
- [ ] cheddar cheese
- [ ] cream
- [ ] cream cheese
- [ ] dip
- [ ] eggs
- [ ] egg substitute
- [ ] feta cheese
- [ ] half & half
- [ ] jack cheese
- [ ] milk
- [ ] mozzarella
- [ ] processed cheese
- [ ] salsa
- [ ] shredded cheese
- [ ] sour cream
- [ ] Swiss cheese
- [ ] whipped cream
- [ ] yogurt
- [ ] _____
- [ ] _____

Seasoning
- [ ] basil
- [ ] bay leaves
- [ ] BBQ seasoning
- [ ] cinnamon
- [ ] cloves
- [ ] cumin
- [ ] curry
- [ ] dill
- [ ] garlic powder
- [ ] garlic salt
- [ ] gravy mix
- [ ] Italian seasoning
- [ ] marinade
- [ ] meat tenderizer
- [ ] oregano
- [ ] paprika
- [ ] pepper
- [ ] poppy seed
- [ ] red pepper
- [ ] sage
- [ ] salt
- [ ] seasoned salt
- [ ] soup mix
- [ ] vanilla extract
- [ ] _____
- [ ] _____

Sauces & Condiments
- [ ] BBQ sauce
- [ ] catsup
- [ ] cocktail sauce
- [ ] cooking spray
- [ ] honey
- [ ] horseradish
- [ ] hot sauce
- [ ] lemon juice
- [ ] mayonnaise
- [ ] mustard
- [ ] olive oil
- [ ] relish
- [ ] salad dressing
- [ ] salsa
- [ ] soy sauce
- [ ] steak sauce
- [ ] sweet & sour
- [ ] teriyaki
- [ ] vegetable oil
- [ ] vinegar
- [ ] _____
- [ ] _____

Drinks
- [ ] beer
- [ ] champagne
- [ ] club soda
- [ ] coffee
- [ ] diet soft drinks
- [ ] energy drinks
- [ ] juice
- [ ] liquor
- [ ] soft drinks
- [ ] tea
- [ ] wine

Paper Products
- [ ] aluminum foil
- [ ] coffee filters
- [ ] cups
- [ ] garbage bags
- [ ] napkins
- [ ] paper plates
- [ ] paper towels
- [ ] plastic bags
- [ ] plastic cutlery
- [ ] plastic wrap
- [ ] straws
- [ ] waxed paper
- [ ] _____

Cleaning
- [ ] air freshener
- [ ] bleach
- [ ] dish soap
- [ ] dishwasher detergent
- [ ] fabric softener
- [ ] floor cleaner
- [ ] glass spray
- [ ] laundry soap
- [ ] polish
- [ ] sponges
- [ ] vacuum bags
- [ ] _____

Personal Care
- [ ] bath soap
- [ ] bug repellant
- [ ] conditioner
- [ ] cotton swabs
- [ ] dental floss
- [ ] deodorant
- [ ] facial tissue
- [ ] family planning
- [ ] feminine products
- [ ] hair spray
- [ ] hand soap
- [ ] lip care
- [ ] lotion
- [ ] makeup
- [ ] mouthwash
- [ ] razors/blades
- [ ] shampoo
- [ ] shaving cream
- [ ] sunscreen
- [ ] toilet tissue
- [ ] toothbrush
- [ ] toothpaste
- [ ] _____
- [ ] _____

Misc. Items
- [ ] batteries
- [ ] charcoal
- [ ] greeting cards
- [ ] light bulbs
- [ ] _____

Today's Agenda

Date: _____

Top Priority

_____
_____
_____
_____

Schedule		Calls
8:00	_____	_____ _____
8:30	_____	_____ _____
9:00	_____	_____ _____
9:30	_____	_____ _____
10:00	_____	_____ _____
10:30	_____	
11:00	_____	
11:30	_____	**Miscellaneous Stuff**
12:00	_____	_____ _____
12:30	_____	_____ _____
1:00	_____	_____ _____
1:30	_____	_____ _____
2:00	_____	_____ _____
2:30	_____	
3:00	_____	
3:30	_____	**Follow-Up**
4:00	_____	_____
4:30	_____	_____
5:00	_____	_____
5:30	_____	_____
6:00	_____	_____

Notes

_____
_____
_____
_____
_____

Today's Agenda

Date: _____

Top Priority

_____
_____
_____
_____

Schedule

8:00 _____
8:30 _____
9:00 _____
9:30 _____
10:00 _____
10:30 _____
11:00 _____
11:30 _____
12:00 _____
12:30 _____
1:00 _____
1:30 _____
2:00 _____
2:30 _____
3:00 _____
3:30 _____
4:00 _____
4:30 _____
5:00 _____
5:30 _____
6:00 _____

Calls

_____ _____
_____ _____
_____ _____
_____ _____
_____ _____

Miscellaneous Stuff

_____ _____
_____ _____
_____ _____
_____ _____
_____ _____

Follow-Up

_____
_____
_____
_____
_____

Notes

_____
_____
_____
_____
_____

Today's Agenda

Date: _____

Top Priority

_____
_____
_____
_____

Schedule	Calls

8:00 _____

8:30 _____

9:00 _____

9:30 _____

10:00 _____

10:30 _____

11:00 _____

11:30 _____

Miscellaneous Stuff

12:00 _____

12:30 _____

1:00 _____

1:30 _____

2:00 _____

2:30 _____

3:00 _____

Follow-Up

3:30 _____

4:00 _____

4:30 _____

5:00 _____

5:30 _____

6:00 _____

Notes

_____
_____
_____
_____
_____

Today's Agenda

Date: _____

Top Priority
_____
_____
_____

Schedule

Time	
8:00	_____
8:30	_____
9:00	_____
9:30	_____
10:00	_____
10:30	_____
11:00	_____
11:30	_____
12:00	_____
12:30	_____
1:00	_____
1:30	_____
2:00	_____
2:30	_____
3:00	_____
3:30	_____
4:00	_____
4:30	_____
5:00	_____
5:30	_____
6:00	_____

Calls
_____ _____
_____ _____
_____ _____
_____ _____
_____ _____

Miscellaneous Stuff
_____ _____
_____ _____
_____ _____
_____ _____

Follow-Up
_____
_____
_____
_____
_____
_____

Notes
_____
_____
_____
_____
_____

Today's Agenda

Date: _____

Top Priority

_____
_____
_____
_____

Schedule

8:00 _____
8:30 _____
9:00 _____
9:30 _____
10:00 _____
10:30 _____
11:00 _____
11:30 _____
12:00 _____
12:30 _____
1:00 _____
1:30 _____
2:00 _____
2:30 _____
3:00 _____
3:30 _____
4:00 _____
4:30 _____
5:00 _____
5:30 _____
6:00 _____

Calls

_____   _____
_____   _____
_____   _____
_____   _____
_____   _____

Miscellaneous Stuff

_____   _____
_____   _____
_____   _____
_____   _____
_____   _____

Follow-Up

_____
_____
_____
_____
_____

Notes

_____
_____
_____
_____
_____

Today's Agenda

Date: _____

Top Priority

_____
_____
_____
_____

Schedule

8:00 _____
8:30 _____
9:00 _____
9:30 _____
10:00 _____
10:30 _____
11:00 _____
11:30 _____
12:00 _____
12:30 _____
1:00 _____
1:30 _____
2:00 _____
2:30 _____
3:00 _____
3:30 _____
4:00 _____
4:30 _____
5:00 _____
5:30 _____
6:00 _____

Calls

_____
_____
_____
_____
_____

Miscellaneous Stuff

_____
_____
_____
_____

Follow-Up

_____
_____
_____
_____
_____

Notes

_____
_____
_____
_____
_____

Today's Agenda

Date: _____

Top Priority

_____
_____
_____
_____

Schedule

8:00 _____
8:30 _____
9:00 _____
9:30 _____
10:00 _____
10:30 _____
11:00 _____
11:30 _____
12:00 _____
12:30 _____
1:00 _____
1:30 _____
2:00 _____
2:30 _____
3:00 _____
3:30 _____
4:00 _____
4:30 _____
5:00 _____
5:30 _____
6:00 _____

Calls

_____   _____
_____   _____
_____   _____
_____   _____

Miscellaneous Stuff

_____   _____
_____   _____
_____   _____
_____   _____
_____   _____

Follow-Up

_____
_____
_____
_____
_____

Notes

_____
_____
_____
_____
_____
_____

Today's Agenda

Date: _____

Top Priority

_____
_____
_____
_____

Schedule

8:00 _____
8:30 _____
9:00 _____
9:30 _____
10:00 _____
10:30 _____
11:00 _____
11:30 _____
12:00 _____
12:30 _____
1:00 _____
1:30 _____
2:00 _____
2:30 _____
3:00 _____
3:30 _____
4:00 _____
4:30 _____
5:00 _____
5:30 _____
6:00 _____

Calls

_____   _____
_____   _____
_____   _____
_____   _____
_____   _____

Miscellaneous Stuff

_____   _____
_____   _____
_____   _____
_____   _____
_____   _____

Follow-Up

_____
_____
_____
_____
_____
_____

Notes

_____
_____
_____
_____
_____
_____

Today's Agenda

Date: _____

Top Priority

_____
_____
_____
_____

Schedule		Calls

8:00 _____   _____ _____
8:30 _____   _____ _____
9:00 _____   _____ _____
9:30 _____   _____ _____
10:00 _____   _____ _____
10:30 _____
11:00 _____

11:30 _____   **Miscellaneous Stuff**

12:00 _____   _____ _____
12:30 _____   _____ _____
1:00 _____   _____ _____
1:30 _____   _____ _____
2:00 _____   _____ _____
2:30 _____
3:00 _____

3:30 _____   **Follow-Up**

4:00 _____   _____
4:30 _____   _____
5:00 _____   _____
5:30 _____   _____
6:00 _____   _____

Notes

_____
_____
_____
_____
_____

Today's Agenda

Date: _____

Top Priority

_____
_____
_____
_____

Schedule

8:00	_____
8:30	_____
9:00	_____
9:30	_____
10:00	_____
10:30	_____
11:00	_____
11:30	_____
12:00	_____
12:30	_____
1:00	_____
1:30	_____
2:00	_____
2:30	_____
3:00	_____
3:30	_____
4:00	_____
4:30	_____
5:00	_____
5:30	_____
6:00	_____

Calls

_____ _____
_____ _____
_____ _____
_____ _____

Miscellaneous Stuff

_____ _____
_____ _____
_____ _____
_____ _____

Follow-Up

_____
_____
_____
_____

Notes

_____
_____
_____
_____
_____

Made in the USA
Middletown, DE
19 November 2018